To

Our lovely neighbours.
Brenda + Colin.

with best wishes

Ron + Joyce.

PICTURE
MY LIFE

Ron Howard
FBIPP

2QT (Publishing) Ltd

First Edition published 2015 by

2QT Limited (Publishing)
Unit 5 Commercial Courtyard
Duke Street
Settle
North Yorkshire
BD24 9RH

Printed by Berforts Information Press Limited

A CIP catalogue record for this book is available from the British Library

ISBN 978-1-910077-55-9

"My love and thanks to Joyce for all of our wonderful years together and without whose support and hours of typing, this book would never have been completed".

CHAPTER ONE

I WAS BORN in May 1925 in Hammersmith, London W6 at no. 19 South Street, fairly near to the River Thames. The dark brown sails of the Dutch ships passing by could be seen from our first-floor window, and the hoot of the coal barges as they neared the Hammersmith Bridge at night on high tide was a common sound.

My mother had eleven children: I was the last. We lived next door to Charlie Vass, who was to become a lifelong friend of mine until he died in 2002. The very old terraced houses had a main sewer that ran straight into the Thames: as a result, water rats were a nuisance in our toilet. When one was heard splashing around in the garden toilet my father would pour boiling water on it to kill it. Otherwise it would have spread its feet in the bowl to prevent being washed away.

Everyone in the road spoke in cockney rhyming slang, and outsiders had some difficulty in understanding what was going on. Mice were seen regularly and had my sisters jumping up on chairs, and many of the houses had wallpaper stuck up with flour paste. This was a haven for bugs (steam tugs in cockney rhyming slang).

I had seven brothers and three sisters: two brothers before me had died young from meningitis. Our loft was crammed with junk. My older brothers would smirk to one another when our old pram was brought down again and dusted. It was a signal that another baby was on its way. This last time, of course, was for me. Hooray!

We had a very long back garden. My brothers would boast that they could throw a stone from the end of the garden into the Thames. The house had a large stone copper for washing our laundry in the scullery. It had a flue leading out into the garden. My mother said she could buy a ha'p'orth of gunpowder with a piece of fuse. This was to blow out the waste blocking the flue into the garden.

Eventually the old houses were pulled down and council flats built on the site. All the builders and bricklayers were a bright and happy lot, always singing 'Danny Boy' and 'In Dublin's Fair City', and of course playing pitch-and-toss in their lunchtime.

Once our house had been pulled down we were able to move into a lovely clean abode. Charlie lived in no. 13 on the second floor - a lucky number for him, as his flat overlooked the Thames and Hammersmith Bridge. On Boat Race day this was a boon. King Street, Hammersmith would be packed with people hoping to get near the riverside and watch Oxford and Cambridge in their yearly race. There would be programme sellers everywhere selling paper flowers and silk lapel favours and noisy clappers. It was sheer bedlam, and shops would be doing a roaring trade.

Hammersmith Bridge, being a suspension bridge, would be closed because the weight of the crowd would have made it collapse. A point of interest was to see the *Stork*, an old boat of Nelson's day moored on the river.

It was used as a training ship for difficult boys. It was always leaking. On the shore there was a permanent tar boiler, and pails full of the molten stuff would be rowed over in a small boat to plug the holes. We boys were told to sniff the smell of tar into our lungs to prevent colds.

The Storky boys, as they were known, always looked smart in their sailor suits. They would be marched with an officer in charge to our school for lessons. After the war the old boat was towed away. It had become a menace to pleasure boats and to the increased barge trade.

Every so often my younger sister would take me to Jerome's portrait studio for a picture in my Sunday best. It was almost a ritual. We would queue up on a Sunday morning and wait for the photographer to call us in. He seemed to make only one exposure and to hope for the best. Then we would call back in three days' time and pay sixpence halfpenny for three postcards. Tinting or sepia was threepence extra.

Over the back of the flats was an old muddy creek. History books say it was there even in Roman times. There was an old wooden bridge over the creek that led to The Dove. This old pub has been famous for many years. Its back garden led out to the Thames, and gave a good view of the river and the boats. The creek entrance had a loading bay for Wiggins-Sankey, the builders' merchants.

When they moved out the ground was covered in old slate and broken bricks. This stuff was useful for our brick fights with the Banin Street gang. They were led by Jamie Livingstone, a tough boy with a wooden leg who could run as fast as any of us. In a scrap his quick fists would punch us to the ground in seconds.

The creek was full of rat holes. Toss a piece of bread in the water and a rat would swim out. It would be easily picked off with a catapult. When hit it would turn over dead, showing its white belly. In those earlier days boys and girls played together, more or less. So teasing girls by picking up an ugly rat and scaring them was common. These water rats had hind legs for swimming. They could not run very fast and, with care, could be picked up. I did this and was bitten. A rat bite meant a trip to the West London Hospital to be cauterised with a hot needle. I still have the big scar on my index finger today.

Our catapults were made from aeroplane elastic bought from Spaldings of Putney. They were always reluctant to sell it for catapults.

Eventually the creek was drained and filled in. Hammersmith Town Hall was built over it. What with Belisha beacons, trolleybuses and a new

Regal Cinema, Hammersmith was doing well. The Regal Cinema was ultramodern – built in the style of art deco. The old cinema, the Blue Hall, was demolished to make way for it.

CHAPTER TWO

My SERIOUS INTEREST in photography began when Charlie Vass came home from school with a picture of him and three other boys hiding behind a classroom door and laughing at Wally Long struggling with his sums. The picture was taken by Mr Munt their maths teacher on an Ensign Selfix folding camera screwed to a wooden tripod. It had a short time exposure despite the darkness of the classroom.

We were both charged with the enthusiasm to buy a camera of our own using our paper round money. Charlie had a big round and earned four shillings a week. For my much smaller round I got two shillings and sixpence. We bought a small box camera from Woolworths. The camera had three parts at sixpence each a part: with a sixpenny Bott film (an own-brand low quality film from Woolworths) the total cost was two shillings. The film was pretty slow and needed good light, and when we could afford it we bought a Selochrome film from the chemist's machine. It cost eleven pence with two halfpennies as change (in a cellophane packet) from the machine.

Woolworths was a haven for young boys when we were growing up. We needed Kolene and Brylcreem for our hair, and some boys had now started shaving. The girls needed Veet for hair removal. We boys could buy a tiny tin of condensed milk for three halfpence. We would pierce two holes in the lid with our penknives and suck out the contents. The taste was sheer heaven. A sixpenny record of Bing Crosby would be played, with him singing his latest hit song, and we would hover around in the store until we had learned most of the lyrics.

I did try many times to get a picture of the Dagenham Girl Pipers. Dressed in their colourful tartans and kilts, these beautiful girls would be frequent visitors to our flats. They were booked by the Reverend Norman Dunning to advertise his meetings at the local Rivercourt Church. He was the original Billy Graham of our time.

I attempted to photograph the girls from my first-floor bedroom window. The screech of pushing the window up alerted the girls' manager to look up, and he saw me with the camera and stopped the girls so that I could take the picture. It was embarrassing because wind kept blowing the curtain over the lens: I was overcome by frustration. I even had the courage to take the picture round to the office of our local paper. The quality obviously wasn't good enough: I heard no more. The Reverend Norman Dunning was a good man of the church: he took a few boys back to Australia to work on his sheep farm. One of these boys wrote to our school to say that the sun never seemed to set in Australia, and that it was seventy miles to the nearest sweet shop.

Our school in Waterloo Street was a lovely school. Every year we would celebrate Empire Day on 24 May. We would sing, 'We hail the flag, the bonnie flag of red and white and blue,' and come home with a hand-held Union flag.

We were compelled to take swimming lessons, what with the school being so near the River Thames. Although we would walk straight to school, we would often return back home walking along the Thameside. On low tide it meant meandering along the riverbank and muddy shoes, followed by a clump round the ear when I got home. Another school gate led out to Marryat Street: its old name was Cutthroat Alley. Its name was changed when, apparently, a murder was committed in a local upholsterer's workshop.

Outside our main gate on a Friday there would always be a rag-and-bone man with lots of goldfish in glass jars. He would shout, 'Goldfish for old rags ... every one a swimmer.' On high tide and in summer months we swam in the Thames near the bridge. We would leave our clothes in a stinky old toilet under the bridge. We would wait in the water for the warm effluent – which was lovely to swim in – to be released from Watney's Brewery. Unfortunately we went home smelling of beer ... another clump!

Sunday school was attended by most children. It was a very pleasant hour. The teacher would give us a text every week: these small religious paper texts were highly valued. One of my brothers would stamp our cards: we would never dare miss a week. Our South Street Mission was run by a lady minister named Sister Lizzie. She was a devoted lady to her community who was also a magistrate, and she was a prolific writer of letters on behalf of her many troubled parishioners.

She organised days out for the children. Twice a year she would book a trolleybus that would run from Hammersmith to Hampton Court for the local kids ... imagine going all that way powered by overhead wires. We would set down in Bushey Park recreation ground and were handed out sandwiches full of awful-tasting sausage meat. We fed this to the deer, and by the time we departed the poor animals were loaded with the stuff.

Nearly always on these excursions there would be an old photographer awaiting the children with his Aptus camera. It was a forerunner to a Polaroid camera. For fourpence halfpenny he would take your photograph by lens cap on a small metal photo plate. The back of the camera would be hooded on a tripod. The metal photo plate would be released into a small tin of developer. It would get a quick wash and a fix, be wiped dry and be handed to you. We were always short of money so he did not do much trade. We had to cross the main road to visit Hampton Court and get lost in the maze.

Early one morning an IRA bomb exploded on Hammersmith Bridge.

The blast cracked some of the windows in our flats. One or two people exaggerated by saying that they had been blown off their beds. Being a suspension bridge it was badly damaged, and was closed for a year.

Charlie and I got a good picture of the double-decker buses loaded with sandbags that were testing the strength of the suspension. We took the picture from the high window in the mansions near the bridge: it seemed to take many days to test the repairs and to ensure that the bridge's load-bearing capacity was unaffected.

Our films were developed and printed by Venables, the local chemist. We also made extra prints ourselves on printout paper (using just window light through the negatives), but these prints lacked contrast. The paper cost three pence for ten sheets, which was much cheaper, but they had to be fixed in proper hypo. The chemist got to know us and gave us his old fixer: that saved us money.

Charlie and I got many of our best pictures of the skaters on Barnes Pond. It would freeze over in winter, and the brightness of the snow gave us perfect negatives.

In Hammersmith we had a soapbox corner in Downes Place where an escape artist would do his best to get out of a straitjacket. There was also Alfred Van Dyn, who was an ex-criminal telling of his experiences in prison. He said that the prisoner in the next cell had murdered a person. He had been told that the last image of the murder remained on the retina of his victim's eyes, so he gouged out his victims' eyes. It was pretty grim listening to this man, and we made sure that we kept our camera out of sight.

The craze for flying Frog aeroplanes swept our flats. These tiny elastic band-powered planes could be bought from Woolworths for sixpence. They were marvellous flyers, keeping in the air for more than a minute. They could also be flown by attaching a small metal cartridge of Jetex fuel. When ignited the aircraft flew higher and much faster. The fuel was also used to prepare skyrockets with a halfpenny banger tied to them to explode high in the air.

We had to be careful not to be caught doing anything dangerous, for we had a regular policeman patrolling our area. This was Constable Hutchins. One day he took our names for kicking a football against the wall of our local telephone exchange. It was a building in the centre of the flats. We were hauled up to the Shepherd's Bush juvenile court, and it brought great shame on our parents.

When living in a close community of council flats you get to know most of the people. My grandmother and my mother were lay midwives: they delivered many babies between them. Some people could not afford a doctor. I could always tell when the new baby was imminent and the piece of catgut was seen suspended in a cupful of Dettol water. This was to tie the umbilical cord. My mother also had the grim task of laying out people who had died. She rarely got paid.

On a Friday and Saturday night Shepherd's Bush Market came alive. Every other stall would have an interesting salesman barking away and demonstrating his wares. Our favourite was the chocolate king, who would open a box of his cheap chocolates and throw them into the crowd and shout that the chocolates came off the back of a lorry – that's why they were so cheap. We boys would nearly get killed in the scuffle to pick up the chocs. Even on a wet night and covered in mud they would go straight into our mouths.

Our favourite comics were the funnies found in the centre pages of American newspapers. Apparently they came over as ballast in regular shipping and were sold by Peterman's, a large second-hand bookshop in the market. We boys would try to shuffle the popular bits into our bargain lot of ten sheets for one penny. Mr Peterman would shout to his son, 'Two ten the ice creams', which meant, 'Keep two eyes and ten fingers on the ice cream freezers (geezers)', to prevent the grab.

Charlie and I felt lucky when his schoolteacher gave us his old folding camera and tripod. It still had the small lens aperture but had three set distances and time exposure. The tripod answered all our prayers: at last we would be able to get good negatives on a dull day. Strange to say, it took some getting used to: there was no tripod screw, so the camera had to be tied with an old scarf. Overexposure in judging the light and the movement of the subjects were our first problems. We finally got the hang of it.

Those early schooldays had their fair measure of illnesses for younger children. Scarlet fever and diphtheria were the most severe. I caught diphtheria and nearly died. I was carted off by ambulance to the Western Fever Hospital on Seagrave Road in Fulham. I was on open order for a time (this meant that I was considered to be close to death) and can vaguely remember my whole family taking turns to come to visit me. The whole group stood around my bed in hoods and white gowns, looking like the Ku Klux Klan. The ward, I remember, had twenty beds – ten on each side – and there were three boys from my own school in the ward.

It was a pretty lively atmosphere as you got better. When we sang, 'Ten green bottles hanging on the wall,' the ward sister would shout, 'Stop. You have got voices like a lot of foghorns.' I then did two weeks' convalescence at Winchmore Hill, then came home with very wobbly legs.

Charlie had become busier with the camera, mainly photographing the local school football teams. This really needed the tripod on dull days.

Rex Regis, who ran the Thameside Boys' Club, told us of a cat that swam across the thirty feet of water to the Chiswick Eyot. We were never lucky enough to catch it. This area was on the walk to Chiswick's open-air swimming pool and we would pass Michael Redgrave's house, which had a very large rounded glass window. We would follow a road to the baths through LEP Transport. It was here that they assembled Opel cars: there was also a lorry dump where they smashed up old vans and lorries. One of the workers regularly gave us huge bags of ball bearings for our catapults. They were so heavy that we had to split them between us to carry home in our handkerchiefs.

The Hammersmith Palace Cinema was converted back to being a music hall again. No more twopenny rush on a Saturday morning, with its serials and cowboy films, plus a bar of toffee on the way out. When the Palace first opened again there were no dressing rooms ready. The appearing artistes changed in houses in the side roads and ran in full make-up to the stage door. We knew one of these landladies, and she asked us to take a picture of her with a group of African tom-tom drummers who were one of the turns on the stage show. They were advertising their appearance in the film *Sanders of the River* with Leslie Banks. Charlie and I were very nervous. We had never been close to black people before this. The men didn't speak English, yet were very happy to pose quickly in the side street for our camera.

One big week for the Palace Theatre was when Reginald Foort appeared on the stage with his giant concert organ. The pipes and stuff arrived in three massive vans with Reginald Foort written on their sides. The sound and vibrations must surely have tested the walls of the old Palace. Our favourite turn was Billy Costello with his Popeye voice.

Photography took a back seat for a while. Charlie and I always looked forward to Bonfire Night on 5 November, so we saved our pennies on a savings card and looked forward to the greatest day of the year. We started to make our own bangers. Most of the chemicals we needed could be bought easily from the chemist. Formulas could be found in some library books, and the monthly magazine called *Spons' Workshop Receipts* gave details on how to make indoor fireworks and signal rockets. For a dollar (four shillings and twopence (4/2d)) formulas could be obtained from America. We boys would pinch railway caps from the signal box on Wormwood Scrubs. These contained mercury fulminate sealed in metal foil. They were placed on the railway line to be detonated as fog warnings as the train wheels crushed them. There was also the old schoolboy favourite, calcium carbide. This rock-like chemical could be bought in sevenpenny tins from any ironmonger's, and was occasionally nicked from post office engineers' bags. It was used in their acetylene blow lamps.

CHAPTER THREE

TIME FOR CHANGE. I became top of the class in my junior school and was sent to a brand-new school in Kensington, opposite the Olympia. While being built this school used the empty classrooms of our junior school to house all their boy scholars, so the teachers were familiar to me. It was the best school in London. It was great for sport, especially cricket, and I was the hundred yards sprint champion.

Dr Cavell was our chemistry master. He would fill a strong bottle with hydrogen and light the gas with a taper. The loud report could be heard throughout the school. When he heard of my interest in explosives he became like a young schoolboy again. He showed me how to make extra-loud Christmas cracker snaps. They would almost blow your arm off when pulled. We had a school orchestra with a violin teacher who was the brother of Gustav Holst, the famous composer.

My nickname at this school was Popeye. It came about because of my interest in the sailor man drawn by the artist E. C. Segar. Not many people would know that he had another girlfriend besides Olive Oyl: her name was Zexa Peal.

At the school the boys preferred American comics. My favourites were *Famous Funnies*, *Tip Top* and *King* comics. These had characters like the Katzenjammer Kids, Smokey Stover, Tilly the Toiler – and Dick Tracy with B.O. Plenty and Buck Rogers.

Even the adverts were interesting, with Mr Coffee Nerves, Clyde Beatty the lion tamer and Humanised Trufood – not forgetting the back pages filled with Daisy air guns and rifles.

The school had organised a school journey to the Peak District. The cost was four pounds, ten shillings ... my brothers had a quick whip-round and I was ready to go. We were told not to bring cameras, as this would cause hold-ups while using them. Two masters hired a Paillard Bolex 16 mm movie camera to cover the trip. We took the steam train to Darley Dale in Derbyshire. Our first outing was to the Blue John mine in Buxton, then on to the Manchester Ship Canal, and we finally visited the Clay Cross ironworks and stone quarry. Our most exciting venture was to the Clay Cross coal mine where we were given miners' helmets fitted with a light on top. We were taken down the pit shaft to the coalface. We looked a grand sight when we came up. We lined up and the movie camera zipped along our faces – but, alas, we never saw the results. The coal mine was privately owned then and the owners gave us a smashing tea of cakes and jam sandwiches. When we got back to school we eagerly awaited the showing of the films of the school journey. They were a washout, and so amateurish a record of our lovely time.

CHAPTER FOUR

THE WAR WAS looming, and we were hoping that our suspicions wouldn't come true. Our school's French master was called to Paris as a translator for our ministers. A picture of our teacher Mr Moss was on the front page of the *Evening News*. It was serious.

Three boys in my class had secured jobs in a Canadian bank. With my knowledge of explosives I myself was destined to become a mining engineer. This didn't come about. War was declared and the air raid sirens started up immediately.

On this particular Sunday morning in September it was a bright sunny day masked by a gloomy mood because of the situation Britain was in. I decided to walk over Hammersmith Bridge and along the towpath to Chiswick Bridge, then through to the Commodore Cinema in Hammersmith. The Commodore was home to Joseph Muscant and his orchestra: he played regularly every Saturday morning on BBC Radio.

On this Saturday there were no people to be seen. It was eerie. The Commodore was showing Judy Garland in *The Wizard of Oz*. I bought a ticket expecting the cinema to be empty, but no. It was packed to the gills with people, and hardly any seats were left. Still, it cheered me up: it was worth the nine pence I paid to get in.

For some reason my mother decided I was not to be evacuated. It was a gloomy time: most boys who were left at home were called upon to fill sandbags. The lovely green fields of Ravenscourt Park were dug up to fill the bags. Filling the bags was a regular daily routine.

I noticed Will Hay the comedian one Sunday morning. He was walking through with a group of Sea Scouts. I had the camera and I stopped him for a picture. He promptly obliged. When the exposure was made he said, 'That won't come out. You had your finger over the lens.'

We were too young to go into the forces and with no schooling I joined the Air Defence Cadet Corps, later to become the ATC. One of our officers, Lt Swarbrick, had been a pilot in the First World War. He had plenty of advice on photography, and had had to use his camera from an open cockpit. He explained how it took all his strength to hold it in the slipstream.

One day when roaming the streets I was stopped by some school inspectors in their car. On learning of my interest in chemistry and explosives they sent me for an interview at Pain's firework factory in Mitcham. Pain's were only making bangers for army training and signal flares, and this didn't interest me.

My father got me a job working in one of Harrods's five engineering shops. He serviced batteries for their electric cars and delivery vans. He was a driver there – first on the petrol vans, then on the electric vans. During the First World War he drove an old gate-change Albion*.

GEORGE 'DUSTY' HOWARD.
Before the First World War he used to take his horse-drawn dustcart full of burnable rubbish down to Battersea Power Station to be burned.

These old vans had no clutch and gears had to be changed by physically forcing them into position with a strong wrist, then hoping for the best. My

---

* Gate-change Albion: Albion Automotive of Scotstoun, Glasgow is a former Scottish automobile and commercial vehicle manufacturer, currently involved in the manufacture and supply of automotive component systems. Although the manufacture of motor cars was the main industry in the first ten years of its existence, it was decided in 1909 to concentrate on the production of commercial vehicles. During World War 1 they built (for the War Office) large quantities of three-ton trucks powered by 32 h.p. engines, using chain drive to the rear wheels. After the war many of these were converted for use as charabancs.

Gate-change Albion

father was known as Dusty because in earlier days he had driven a horse-drawn dustcart. It was a massive horse, and he won many prizes with it at the Regent's Park exhibitions. His job was to carry burnable rubbish along the embankment to Lots Road Power Station at Battersea.

I had four brothers and a sister working at Harrods: we were virtually running the place. Brother Alf was in telephone orders to begin with. He upset a lady on the phone one day and she ordered him to be sacked. As a consequence he was moved to the electrical department on sales. Brother George was in furniture removals, brother Frank was in upholstery on piecework, brother Bill was in fruit and veg – and my sister Ada was in the sanctions office, dealing with bad debts.

Harrods had sixty modern electric vans and sixty petrol vans. The electric vans had a limited range of miles (in relation to their battery size). Town vans with A4 batteries would cover forty miles a day: A6 batteries would do sixty miles (a little further afield). Petrol vans would cover the suburban areas. They would also have a porter – a man who would sit with the driver and do all the legwork to the customer's door.

My father's round dealt mainly with the City of London. He would load his van in Pavilion Road, and from his little cubbyhole on the bank he would play popular tunes on his mandolin for twenty minutes. While the men on this working bank were loading up they would frequently get a visit and a greeting from Sir Richard Burbidge, whose family owned Harrods at that time.

Harrods was self-supporting in its energy: they had sunk their own artesian wells, so there was no shortage of water. The electricity came from giant generators in the basement, which supplied a 200-volt circuit. Therefore all normal 230-volt appliances were a little underpowered.

There were five engineering workshops in this giant store. The carpenters' shop fixed all the woodwork and furniture, the plumbing shop looked after all the waterworks and the van shop (my shop) serviced all the transport vehicles. The lift shop serviced the lifts and escalators. This last shop repaired and rewound all coils, armatures and electrical appliances. Then there were the engineers' stores with tools, screws, light fittings and so on. The building side was partly run by McAlpine's, but the war ended their connection.

Harrods had its own tea blending and tea packing floor in Trevor Square. There were shoe repairs, a chocolate factory and a bakery scattered over the various floors. Trevor Square was a hive of industry. In the vicinity there was the car hire service at Cheval Place, with customer garaging in Cadogan Place. Montpelier Place was known for cooking and preparing banquets, and all the utensils were stored here. A mile away was Draycott Avenue, the petrol van garage and fill-up station. It was also a very large warehouse for storing furniture.

Jesse Bridge was the foreman of the Trevor Square van shop. Mr Bridge foresaw the oncoming war and the shortage of petrol, so he designed a van of simple structure that could be manufactured on the grounds of the Barnes depositories. This large Thameside piece of land housed plant nurseries and had a skid patch for training drivers of these new vehicles. Even I learned to drive here. There were no gears on them – just a lever to push for speed and a brake – and only road experience was needed.

Electric vans were not new by any means: plenty of the old-type factory-driven vehicles were lined up at Barnes. They were kept as museum pieces. I was assigned to be Ernie Cowley's electrician mate in the Trevor Square van shop. I would be topping up batteries and mending faulty windscreen wipers, and I was amazed at the skills of the van engineers. Old George Parsons taught me how to anneal and case-harden bearings, and how to make a hacksaw blade last ten times longer. Sadly, a bomb dropped on his fire watch post and killed him.

Lead burning taught me how to solder my mum's leaking kettles at home. Ernie Cowley was a very clever man. To me he was a genius, especially in chemistry. He would assess the age of batteries and the life of the electrolyte. He was also an expert at timing petrol and diesel engines. We got together on making nitrogen triiodide and sprinkled tiny grains of it over the shop floor, and had it cracking and popping under the feet of the other engineers. One night a test tube full of the stuff automatically exploded and wrecked our little wire-caged laboratory. This little room was used to check the specific gravity of the large alkaline van batteries.

Best of all, Ernie was an enthusiastic photographer. He had a Zeiss Ikon folding camera with an f4.5 Tessar lens. His album of photos made me realise the intelligence of subject arrangement in a picture. They were much more than just snaps.

He also regularly took portraits of the breakdown crews – the men on overtime who would be waiting for the phone call from a driver whose batteries had run out. If it was in the blackout the driver would have difficulty finding a phone box and proving where he was situated. This was a pretty regular occurrence. Meanwhile – after breaking up the breakdown crews' card games – Ernie would set up his photofloods in his Selo folding reflectors and shoot off a couple of films.

He too had seen the war coming and had stocked up with plenty of 120 films. I enjoyed picking up his prints from the photographic department: I could then see at first hand the results, which were always clear and sharp. This got me going again, and I had to buy a better camera. Fortunately I had a very kind older sister, Nellie, who was doing well on war work (welding aircraft seats). She put up the money for the new camera and Ernie and I walked round to Dollond & Aitchison to buy a similar camera to his, but with the cheaper 4.5 Triotar lens and no rangefinder. It cost seven pounds ten shillings, including six 120 films. I soon used them up.

One of the great problems was obtaining 120 films. I had family, friends and scouts everywhere searching around for out-of-date stuff and even 620 films that could be easily adapted, and I was on the waiting lists of all the local shops who could have sold photographic goods.

One day I was lucky: I found a machine full of Selochrome 120s. It was on the wall of a chemist's shop in Lowndes Square (just off Sloane Street), and the packets still had the two halfpennies change in them. I began borrowing money and unloading the machine day by day. Soon there were just six left, but when I popped round to get them the shop had been bombed the night before. The machine was still hanging loosely on the wall. The area was taped off, and firemen were scrambling over the ruins.

My poor old films were hanging there untouchable, for looting during the war was said to be punishable by death. Eventually the supply of 120 films dried up completely, so it was back to changing the camera so that it could take 116 films. Fortunately 116 was not a popular size, so films were slightly easier to obtain.

My camera was a Kodak Autographic with a light, tight slot on the back so that you could title your snaps with a point on autographic film. The lens was a lovely sharp f6.8 Goerz Dagor lens. It took eight larger pictures (four and a quarter by two and a half inches) on 116 pan film. I had to get used to the boss-eyed viewfinder while correcting for parallax. I fixed a supplementary lens for close-up portraits and used a tape measure to the sitters' noses every time. I got lovely clear results with it screwed to an old Gandolfi tripod and became very busy ... I made sure I was careful during the blackout, and used photofloods on dark nights. It seemed that every soldier wanted pictures of his loved ones.

I bought an Envoy three and a half by two and a half enlarger and made a makeshift darkroom in our bathroom in Riverside Gardens. I used my mother's large pastry board across the bath to support it. Enlarging paper had to be searched for, and films had to be seesawed through MQ developer – the same mix used for the paper. I had an Ilford red safelight for films and an orange safelight for paper. The bathroom door had to be opened every so often to let in air, as one time I had fainted through lack of air.

I was very grateful for my life in the van shop because I was working with two remarkable men. Ernie Cowley never swore or used any sort of bad language. The other man was Bob Moss. Bob was taken from McAlpine's the builders. His job in the van shop was to top up the batteries and repair worn-out cells. This called for renewing the plates on lead-burning new connectors.

Bob was a very funny man. He was a comedian: his utterings and joking would make Sammy Cahn look like an amateur. He would have a quick nap in one of the furniture vans in the afternoon. One day he didn't wake up and got carried to Guildford before the driver realised he was there. Every day I looked forward to working with him.

Bob worked at weekends at the Chelsea Palace music hall – he pulled the curtains after the acts. One day he came in beaming, saying he had got me my first professional job photographing a singer called Judah Elboz (who was appearing at the Palace that week). On that inauspicious Friday night the bombing was heavy: the no. 11 bus was not running and trains were doubtful. Cycling would have been murder with all the camera gear, so I lost the job. Still, I got the pleasure of getting Bob's fourpenny-halfpenny bacon sandwich from the cafe across the road in Trevor Square. He always complained that the bacon had been cut with a razor blade. I will never forget him.

Nothing seemed to deter the spirit of the people in wartime. The bombing of London did not prevent shows being put on: they still went ahead with their programmes. You could sit in a cinema and hear the ack-ack guns making a noisy racket outside.

My enthusiasm for photography ran through the van shop like wildfire. I was being compared with Howard Coster (a well-known local photographer on Buckingham Palace Road). The van shop needed a little building up, because it was held in low esteem due to our pongy overalls. Working under the vans brought us into contact with the odd pile of horse manure, as many breweries were reverting to the horse and cart to save petrol.

It was a misery getting home from work in the evening. I wasn't allowed to stay at work after four o'clock. When they arrived at Knightsbridge the Tube trains would be already full of passengers, and people had to fight to get out of the train. The doors would jam and it was a struggle to get home. Even when you got home it was gloomy, especially on dark nights. Our air raid shelters were quite inadequate. Tobacco smoke fouled the air, young children would be crying – and only a limited number of people used them. It was always better to take a chance and sleep in your own bed. When the German bombers could be heard and the anti-aircraft guns got going it must be said that few people needed laxatives. My family were no braver than anybody else. All over the flats toilet chains could be heard being pulled. In fact in the whole of the twenty years we lived in the flats I never saw a plumber being called: the cisterns were pretty robust.

When a bomb was dropped people seemed to instinctively know its location. We young boys would ghoulishly set out to see for ourselves the extent of the damage and report back. A small German bomb whistled through the air one night and dropped right on my sister's place of work. It was very accurate, and reduced the place to matchwood. This tiny factory was only making ambulance bells.

When I was asleep one night my whole double-sized bedroom window was blown out. This left me sleeping in the moonlight. An air raid warden climbed up to the window to confirm that I was safe in bed. The window was easily put back the next day, with the hole covered in hardboard. The council builders were marvellous. When the window was open I was able to take an unofficial photo of all the missing slates on the opposite roofs. In the midst of all of this I still kept my paper round going, though the news itself was only on a single sheet of paper. I had to catch the workman's special train before seven thirty for three pence (the price doubled after that time).

Eventually Ernie Cowley was called up to become a navigator in the RAF. I envied him, and realised that I had lost a great friend and mentor. The van shop didn't seem the same, and it was no longer any place for me.

I was still too young to join the forces, but I heard from an old schoolmate that you could get into the RAF even if you were under the right age by working as an apprentice on the aero engines at Horton aerodrome. I arranged to see him, and a bomb blast killed him where we were supposed to meet. This seemed to upset my nervous system and I became a victim of trauma, memory loss and tiredness. I had signed on at Hounslow registry for the forces, and they sent me to the Mill Hill emergency hospital for treatment. Mill Hill public school had been evacuated, and was being used as a rehabilitation hospital. It was run by the military, and the nurses there were very special: they lived up to their reputation of being angels. All the rehabilitation things were there for us to do: basket making, pottery, whist drives... We even had a visit from Lancelot Vining, a *Daily Mirror* photographer who at the time was writing a weekly column in the *Amateur Photographer.*

I was able to use my camera, and was given a broom cupboard to use as a darkroom. I managed to take many portraits of the soldiers and airmen for their families. I could only make contact prints: it was home from home. Very ill patients were put to sleep with somniphan and were fed through the nose. When woken up it was hoped that they would have forgotten most of their troubles. Another treatment was an insulin injection early in the morning. By ten o'clock the patient was ravenous for food and was given plenty of bread, butter and jam. It was considered that putting on weight could be a cure for their ailments. The hospital was run on a military basis: the Army Physical Training Corps took care of their fitness.

It must have been September, as Cox's apples were on sale. The local cinema was free to all hospital patients. I popped in one very hot afternoon to see Abbott and Costello in *Rio Rita*. There were only a couple of others in there besides myself: the place was empty. The hospital seemed to clear up my problems after seven weeks. My doctor's name was Gillespie. He said, 'No going into the forces yet. Let's see if Harrods will take you back with a job to follow your hobby.' Sure enough, I was snapped up by the Harrods studio: they needed a camera assistant.

CHAPTER FIVE

Mr Harold Young was the chief operator at the Harrods studio. I remember him saying, 'There is no money in photography unless you are at the top.' I wasn't too concerned by this remark as I saw myself becoming a photographer for the RAF, although it did make me think.

Photography at the time was a new and luxurious field of work. Working in the beautiful Harrods studio, surrounded by wonderful pictures and the lush glamour of it all ... to a young sixteen-year-old it was Utopia. Maybe it was here that I lost my ambition to go into the forces. Taking real portraits was in my blood, and Mill Hill proved that there was another life in Civvy Street. In any case I was still keeping up my Morse code in the ATC, and some boys were being directed straight into the navy.

The Harrods studio was situated in a long hallway that led to the Georgian Restaurant on the fourth floor. The walls had large 24 x 20 inch prints of brigadiers, air commodores and admirals – plus wonderfully arranged ladies at court, dressed in the most beautiful drapes. This was photography of a class that could only be afforded by the wealthy.

These very special photographs, I learned, were printed by Scotts of Ealing on Kodak Kodura paper. This firm also specialised in quality copying and framing. This new job meant a change of times, and starting later on in the day meant that I would be able to travel to work by cycle. It was a straight route through Cromwell Road, Earls Court and Great Church Lane, then into Hammersmith. The traffic was negligible due to petrol rationing, and it took only twenty minutes on the bike. I would take the route back via Kensington High Street past the Albert Hall. A straight run: no hold-ups. One morning I met my older brother pushing a car along the Great Church Lane. The woman driver had run out of petrol, and I jumped off my bike to help him. We pushed her a good quarter of a mile, and had to leave her to get back to work. She shrieked and swore at us for leaving her stranded, as there were no petrol stations in Hammersmith.

My job in the studio was to prepare the camera ready for Mr Young so that he could press the rubber bulb to make an exposure. It was quite a routine, and needed good eyesight. The camera was a massive structure made by Kodak: it had to be pushed around on boxwood feet on a lush carpet. The camera was so heavy that there could be no camera shake: the exposure would be fairly generous for the slow Kodak orthochromatic film (700 H and D).

For a portrait I would push the camera into position, then open the Dallmeyer shutter to focus on the sitter's eyes with the aid of a magnifier. If it was a three-quarter-length shot I would have to make sure that the hands and eyes were in focus by adjusting the camera movements. When everything looked ready I would lock focus on the movements and close the shutter with the bulb release. Then the dark slide would be pushed in, the sheath withdrawn – and the finger click would signal Mr Young to do his stuff. The slide would then be pushed along for a second exposure.

The Kodak camera was originally a 12 x 10 masked down to a half plate. Even that was masked to give two exposures on half-plate film (a normal sitting would be eight exposures (four films)). Very important people would get a full half plate or even 10 x 8 films (very rarely, though).

The camera lens was a Taylor-Hobson-Cooke fourteen-inch 5.6 Aviar lens. It was stopped down a little to give extra quality. Exposures seemed to be from about one fifth to one tenth of a second. Orthochromatic film gave rise to an exaggeration of pimples and spots (all of which had to be removed by retouching) due to its insensitivity to their colour. Mr Young always seemed to be in a pitched battle with ladies when he asked them to remove some of their lipstick. They were told it would look like black tar if left on.

After the sitting I would unload the dark slides into a safety box (ready for developing). The studio lighting was from three banks of four mercury vapour strip lights. They were hung from the ceiling to give the main actinic light for the blue-sensitive orthochromatic film. The modelling light was a yellow sodium bulb in a large reflector. The bulb was cupped to reflect diffusely on to the sitter. There was a Mull Richardson ceiling spotlight with side mirrors to light their hair. The background was a variety of coloured curtains and sprayed boards.

To avoid reflections in their spectacles customers would be given glassless frames. I would pop down to the optical department for the nearest-match frames. Films were developed in Kodak Time Standard developer, which gave the very high-contrast negatives needed for the diffused light of the Sichel enlarger. The ladies' hair would be tidied in the hairdressing department, which was next door.

Occasionally I would be asked to search for very old negatives in the stockroom above the studio. This room was an Aladdin's cave – not only did it store old plates, it contained all the studio paraphernalia of the past. There were backgrounds, lenses, drapes and old lighting stands with spotlights. I found some boxes of 16 x 20 glass plates of wedding groups, in which every face had noticeably had some retouching. I did ring up Kodak recently to ask if I was dreaming about the size of these plates. No one could give me a straight answer. Nobody at Kodak was sure what orthochromatic film was and why it would be used for portraits.

A group of weddings was taken by the studio. I remember that the bride and groom were portrayed on a staircase in the family home of one of the directors of Harrods. Lighting and large amounts of diffuser muslin were taken to the house in a large Harrods hire purchase van. I travelled in the back of the van in a deckchair with the light on. I was not allowed in the house. I had little knowledge as to where we were. I had memories of the superb photographs with the subjects standing at the bottom of the large staircase.

There was news for the studio when the Harrods amateur developing and printing department had to close. The customers had dried up through the shortage of film and Ethel Ingrams (who ran the department) came to help in the studio. As a result we benefited by taking over paper and film quotas, which introduced Barnet material. Barnet also supplied their own orthochromatic film and very thin airmail paper, which was useful for passports. I myself was allowed to take the odd portrait in the studio, using old boxes of pre-war sample films. There was a good supply of this out-of-date material stacked away under the darkroom sink. There was also an old box of 16 x 20 Illingworth paper. It was sepia-toned and was used as a base for oil or watercolour portraits.

Mr Young had trained as a photographer in a Paris studio. He could speak French perfectly well, though we never had any French customers. He certainly looked the part with his white hair and his goatee beard, which was regularly trimmed in the men's hairdressing department to keep up his appearance. He was chief photographer at Lenare's studio in Bond Street. They were famous for their fog pictures, which were so called due to their excessive use of diffusers. He was also a breeder of Pomeranians and was well known at the Kennel Club. He would occasionally have one of these toy dog owners bring their Poms into the studio to be photographed. This meant piling on the light for a short exposure. Four legs had to be shown, with the dog looking up in profile: not easy with the big camera.

One day I took my Soho Reflex in to photograph a dog on fast pan film. With a shorter shutter speed it gave a sharper result and a lovely clear print of the animal. It fell on blind eyes: no young upstart was going to change the system.

Thomas Fall of Baker Street would be Harrods's nearest rival: he was a real expert on every type of animal. Johnny Johnson was the studio printer, and he was a very proud Scotsman. He could play the bagpipes and sing all the Harry Lauder songs. He gave up his flat in nearby Walton Street to live in the large fire watch post on the roof of Harrods. As a result he became an air raid warden as well.

Johnny wore his kilt only in the evenings, and was a master at darkroom printing. He used no timers or clocks: he just made the exposures under the enlarger by counting himself. Then after a large batch was exposed he would slip twenty or thirty prints at a time in a deep dishful of MQ developer. The prints would be perfectly exposed when developed, then thrown over into an acetic acid stop bath before he transferred them to the fixer. The fixer was plain hypo crystals dissolved in water with a spoonful of metabisulphate.

Proofs were given a short wash only. Finished prints were washed for an hour, then hung up face down on muslin drying racks. The prints were sponged off to remove any spots of rust or bits that might be in the artesian water, then blotted and placed on the frames of the drying racks. In the morning the dry prints were sorted into their batches to be scrutinised by Mr Young. One or two extra prints would be made on a large order and the worst thrown out.

The giant 12x10 Sichel enlarger was wall-mounted and counterweighted so that it was easily moved up and down with a simple arm movement, then locked. The large lamp house contained an M-shaped mercury vapour tube that gave even light through diffused glass. For the smaller half-plate negatives it was perfect (some shading was needed for larger negatives). As the lamp took ten minutes or so to warm up the light was not turned off during short breaks.

After a few months of burning the enlarger tube blackened up and had to be cleaned by the makers. I was given the very pleasant task of taking the tube to Hewittics of Hersham. The glass tube was tied by soft straps to the inside of a protective wooden crate and wasn't heavy. Although of teenage years I had not set foot out of London on my own before, so this was going to be an exciting trip.

I was given the money to buy my rail ticket at Victoria Station and, carrying an awkward package, I took off to Hersham. I arrived at Hewittics after walking for – seemingly – miles from the station. The workers made a great fuss of me: I had tea and cakes, and the name of Harrods carried me along. I think it was a rare sight to see a youth who should have been in the forces out working.

When I boarded the train back to London there were no seats. The carriages were chock-a-block – full of soldiers and sailors on leave from Portsmouth and Salisbury. They viewed my precious open crate with amazement and suggested it looked like one of Hitler's secret weapons. The train was so packed that I couldn't even sit down on the crate in the corridors. I eventually got back to the store safely.

In between the customer sittings I learned about negative retouching. There were four retouching windows in the darkened retouching room. The pencils had soft, medium and hard black leads. These were kept to a fine point with sandpaper. The Barnet film had a matt backing that helped the pencil and needed little retouching medium.

The finishing room was very large. It was run by Miss Bottle, whose husband was the chief camera operator at Van Dyke Studios in Victoria. She worked with a fine brush and black watercolour paint. The print was then sprayed with gum to hide any brush marks. She also signed every print with the famous Harrods logo. Miss Chambrey was a newcomer finisher from a Northampton studio. Her work was frowned on at first because she used pencil on the prints. However, she was very good and soon settled into the team. Miss Brand and Miss Tomlinson were the mounters and framers and took care of the posting and packing. Enid Bell was the main negative retoucher: she shared the workload with Mr Satterthwaite.

Sat, as we called him, came up from East Sussex every Tuesday and Friday. He was a relief fireman in his village and he worked in the retouching room on the Tuesday: he left fairly early and took a large batch of work home with him to bring back on the Friday.

Mrs Churchill (the wife of Winston Churchill) came into the store one day with her secretary (who had previously had a passport sitting as a test run on her behalf). They were enquiring as to whether a passport of Mrs Churchill could be taken straight away. It was one of Mr Young's days off with his dogs, so Johnny Johnson had to operate the session instead of him.

So the great lady was booked in immediately, and Miss Tomlinson (a receptionist) did the camera work. The passports were a great success: they were very flattering because they were taken with the sitter seated a long way from the camera. This would give a small head on the negative (suitable for contact printing). The size had to be one inch from the top of the head to the chin. Little retouching was needed. Shortly afterwards Mrs Churchill booked a proper sitting, with Mr Young taking care of all the photography. The negatives were carefully retouched and printed, and I didn't see any of the results. The whole thing was cloaked in mystery: everyone was so secretive. When Mrs Churchill came to see the proofs there was complete chaos. She hated the pictures. She said that they made her look like a woman of the streets (I dare not say the word she said). The whole workplace was in shock, because they thought the pictures were marvellous. The proofs were torn up and the negatives destroyed. My own assessment was that the orthochromatic film was inclined to give a leathery look to a mature face. No amount of retouching can remove that. Mrs Churchill was a very attractive lady: no doubt about that.

Mr Young had a very good friend in one of Harrods's important customers. He was an older man, and was always visiting the studio because of his interest in Pomeranians. This customer was very kind to me when he gave me a tapestry for a background (he knew by now that I was taking photographs of my own friends and relatives).

I still have this tapestry, though I have misused it many times. When my old Ford Popular was stuck outside in the road (we had no garage) I laid it under the car bonnet to keep the engine from freezing in cold weather. Once or twice I drove the car some distance before realising that the tapestry was there.

Mr Young, I could tell, was not happy with my relationship with this man. One day he asked me to accompany him to the record department. We sat in a recording booth and he asked my opinion on his purchase of the *Warsaw Concerto* by Richard Addinsell. This lovely melody featured in the film *Dangerous Moonlight*.

An abrupt change came in the studio when Johnny Johnson was ordered to give up the darkroom printing. He had metal poisoning, as he would not use gloves when developing the prints: his fingers had swollen up like Cumberland sausages and his nails had dropped off.

I was asked to take over the printing, and I took to it like a duck to water. At first Miss Ingram helped me put over the prints to the fixer. Then I managed everything on my own. All the pictures of men had a number one diffuser on the enlarging lens: the ladies had a number two (heavier) diffuser. Full lengths and groups were never diffused.

All the printing paper came in boxes of 16 x 20 and was cut down to the various smaller sizes. It was the economical way. The lovely Kodura paper was no longer available: it contained too much silver content (silver was in short supply). Kodapal replaced it. This came in single weight – again, for economy – and, as a result, was easier to mount.

Ilford were keen on getting in to the Harrods studio, and offered a trial supply of Plastica paper. It was tried out as proof paper because it had a greeny tinge. It was a chlorobromide paper that when taken a little darker in printing could be brought back to sparkling life with a rub of ferricyanide. Guess what? Many customers preferred it to Kodapal despite the green tinge.

In pre-war days the studio operated an album scheme. For twenty-one guineas a child would be given a yearly photograph with a free sitting. This was a good deal for parents, but naturally the studio profited from the sales that came alongside this scheme. These beautiful albums were made by Barton's of Birmingham.

The studio sold oil colour portraits by Mr De Luca and Mr Rowley for thirty-five guineas. An ivory cameo miniature would cost ninety-six guineas: a good price, considering that you could buy a three-storey house in Shepherd's Bush for a hundred pounds.

Great excitement would be caused if a popular celebrity was seen in the store. Phones would ring all around and coats would be thrown on, and a dignified rush down the back stairs to see this personality would ensue. There was a feeling of great pride when groups of American officers were seen in the shop ... to think that these men in their very classy uniforms came to help us fight the common enemy.

A simple MQ developer was made up one gallon at a time then diluted one to three with water. Eventually the processes were simplified and Johnson's Azol was used for film and paper. It contained amidol and was diluted nine to one. It was easy to use. However it did have an unpleasant smell and, combined with the sometimes strong smell of the artesian water, the darkroom became pretty pongy.

Ted Stark took over from me as the camera operator. Ted was a Barnado's boy. He was fascinated by the darkroom and wanted to print some of his own negatives. I told him that he would have to find his own paper if there was a large number to do. To my surprise, when I came back from lunch the tray containing a solution of hypo was full of Basildon Bond writing paper (bought in the stationery shop downstairs). He had thought that the mystical blue light of the enlarger had the magic effect on any paper.

I was still in the Air Training Corps. One good friend, John Corsini, was doing a night's fire watch stint in Earls Court Road and asked me to join him. Shops paid seven shillings per night for people to do the duty for them. It was good money.

My shop was WHSmith. The manager of the shop was very glad to have me take over his duty. He also ordered my copies of *The Saturday Evening Post*: it was a refreshing American magazine with front covers of paintings by Norman Rockwell. These paintings gave many ideas to photographers to copy. It was a fortnightly magazine, and when not available the manager would tell me that the boat bringing over supplies was sunk by U-boats. I still wonder where he got this information. Such were the stories of war.

The fire watch post had large rooms that were useful as a studio for taking the photographs of many of the lads in their ATC uniforms. On warm nights John and I would sleep outside on the first-floor door portico. We would come inside if there was any danger of shrapnel falling. We risked rolling off the portico – a drop of fifteen feet into the front garden.

John and I also had a little bit of show business in our blood. Every night the Kensington Odeon would hold a collection in the cinema for the RAF Association. We would also do a little magic turn by asking a member of the audience their first name, and I would tap it out in Morse code on a tambourine. John, way down on the stage, would then call out the name. It went down well to loud clapping.

One day – when returning to work on my bike – the air raid siren started blasting. I was tootling along Kensington High Street when I heard a buzz bomb. I could see it coming straight for me along the Earls Court Road. It stopped and dived and I lay down in the road. There was hardly any traffic.

It struck a little Lyons Corner House fifty yards or so away. I was covered in dust, and bits of wood were falling for ever. Shop windows were blown out and glass was everywhere. Dresses and shoes were lying in the road, and there was not a soul in sight. I picked myself up and pedalled off to work. When I got to the studio Mr Young viewed my messy clothes and sent me back home. I am sure that he was thinking more about his negatives becoming covered in dust than my health. I would much rather have got on with my printing: being home in the afternoon was such a bore. Next day had to be a visit to the quack's. That meant seeing Dr Dobie Bateman on the fourth floor. Her very loud voice could be heard well before you reached the clinic.

Whenever my call-up papers came along it would mean that I would have to go to Hounslow for medical assessment. Although I passed the test as A1 (fit for service) Mr Young replied on my behalf, saying that my work at Harrods was essential as it was dealing mainly with the forces. I was ordered to work two days per week in a small workshop in Sloane Street where large reconnaissance blow-ups were being printed for the RAF. The smell of acetic acid was very strong. I wasn't there for long.

The Canadian air force took over the fifth floor of the Harrods store. The Canadians had a tremendous feeling of loyalty to this country. It seemed that most had Scottish ancestry so they were friends of Johnny Johnson, and they joined him in many a sing-song and dance on his fire watch post. Going out for a drink with the Canadians was a pleasure: they believed in having a kitty for paying for drinks. Our stupid rounds system didn't suit them. 'Spread the load,' they would say. They were great party lovers, and had access to a little more booze and spirits than we poor old English. Johnny had a whale of a time dancing Scottish reels with the Canadian girls. They were always singing 'Solid Sam', the flip side to Glen Miller's 'Holiday for Strings'.

I read the *Amateur Photographer* each week: it kept me in touch with adverts for cameras and sales of materials. You had to be lucky to make a deal because an advert took six to seven weeks to appear. By the time you wrote off to an advertiser the article had been sold.

I met George Irving through one of these adverts: he was a train driver on the Northern Line. On Sundays he ran a studio on the Hanworth Road, Hounslow. He had a display of his photos in a showcase standing in the front garden. He was always fully booked up by the American lads from a local airbase. I would cycle over and take most of the portraits on his adapted Sanderson camera, using a lens cap. He used Barnet card negatives and printed on a reflection enlarger. One of his advertising features was to say that I, a Harrods photographer, would be taking the pictures. Every Sunday I looked forward to it. Weddings he covered himself. He got by using out-of-date roll film and anything he could find plate-wise. He was the one who bought the house on Elmo Road, W12.

One day a phone call came for me to the Harrods studio. We were not allowed phone calls, so I knew it had to be something very urgent. A Mr H. S. Anthill of the Harrow Road was ringing to say that his tender to photograph a number of people killed in a fire had been accepted by his council. The fire was caused by a bomb in an intense air raid ... could I help him that evening? He seemed very nervous and pleaded with me, saying that this job would help him get an extra quota of photographic material. I was to meet him at Green Park station at six o'clock. I cycled home hurriedly, swallowed my dinner, and got to the station as soon as I could.

He was waiting by his bunk on the Underground station. He was with his girlfriend. They both used the station as an air raid shelter: she had the bunk above his. There were four carrier bags of light bulbs, camera bits, assorted wires, a tripod and a changing bag. We left the girlfriend there and got on the train, changing at Gloucester Road, and on the Inner Circle to Kensington High Street station.

We walked across to Church Road to find the church, where the bodies were kept in the crypt. The air was a bit whiffy, and a lady from the local hospital was there to help us unwrap the shrouds and clean the faces.

Some were burnt, and crackled when the flannel touched them. The tripod at its lowest was difficult to manoeuvre, and when the 500-watt bulb was switched on it blew the church fuses. Fortunately the caretaker repaired them quickly by torchlight.

It was a sombre experience. These people and children had died in the fire in a local block of flats, which was caused by a bomb in an intense air raid. The faces were recorded on paper negatives, exposed by a lens cap. I changed the exposed slides in a changing bag. Mr Antill asked me to help him the next day as well, but I refused.

The trains had stopped for the evening and I had to make my way home from the church in a thick blackout. I ran most of the way. When I got home I had a job to stop shivering. I was glad to get to work the next day. The studio was a very happy place. Miss Winter was there as usual, arguing with a lady customer over the change of her husband's rank. The pips on the shoulder of his proofs needed to be altered up to his higher rank by retouching for the final prints. Such were the delays in producing the finished order. It was not easy to change the shoulder pips, especially on the far shoulder. That would be out of focus. Johnny Johnson was the expert.

On the wide pavement outside the Natural History Museum, which was just down the road, there was a large independent display of portraits by Paul Tanqueray. The displays were in two large cases in the centre of the pavement. They were mainly theatre portraits of actors and actresses, showing tilted heads and bizarre backgrounds. Mr Young was quite furious when I okayed the photography. 'Don't copy that rubbish,' he said. 'It will get you nowhere.'

My younger sister was always critical of my photography, saying that it would be a long while before I could reach the standard of Harrods. Just to fool her I got Miss Bottle to sign one of my best photographs of a Canadian girl in uniform. The Harrods logo did the trick. My sister said, 'When you get this good you know you have made it.' I let her down gently, though afterwards she did remark she wasn't completely fooled.

I was leaving the store at four o'clock one afternoon when there was a loud staccato bang. Looking up, there in the clear blue sky was a puff of white smoke. It was miles up, and I quickly realised that it was a German V-2 rocket exploding on entering the earth's atmosphere. There was no defence, it seemed, against this new wartime peril. However, the war was coming to an end and I was coming to the end of my time in the Harrods studio. It was time for a change.

I had met Charles Adams through his buying and selling adverts in the *Amateur Photographer*. He too was looking for a change. He was the photo layout designer for *Picture Post*. He was starting a wedding business and needed help to rig up a darkroom in his private house in Streatham. Charles had been wheeling and dealing with 35 mm film reloads and camera exchanges. When I told him of my Harrods wages he immediately said, 'I will double it.'

CHAPTER SIX

CHARLES HAD BEEN a wartime fireman, and had picked up many contacts. This had led to him starting to photograph Sunday synagogue weddings. He also had contacts for taking the photographs for Masonic dinners. While Charles was waiting for his father's premises to be adapted I had to get temporary work. First I had a lovely job working in press photography darkrooms. Then I had a job printing cinema stills for a firm in Holborn. This firm used huge amounts of photographic paper, and their girls were glazing prints all through the night.

Eventually Charles moved into his father's premises on Liverpool Road, Islington. Mr Adams senior and Charles's brother Jack were true craftsmen. They made process cameras for Littlejohn's the process engravers. They were making posters for advertising boards, and used giant cameras big enough for a child to stand in. To see them planing the thin slats of wood needed for the dark slide covers was truly amazing.

Charles was a first-class photographer. His favourite cameras were Zeiss Contaxes and Contaflexes with f1.5 Sonnar lenses. These cameras were inclined to have their focal plane shutters slow up in very cold weather.

I used his 16 on Super Ikonta for weddings. I liked the larger-size negatives – and the super-sharp lens it had, which was perfect for taking the groups. Charles used 35 mm all the time. He would often take a large group in two halves to make sure that everybody was clearly seen. Not all photographers used 35 mm on weddings – but Charles was an innovator and realised that many more intimate pictures could be taken, which increased the sales of his photographs. The Ilford HP3 film had just enough speed to cover the pictures around the dinner tables during the Masonic functions. Sometimes shutter speeds were down to one tenth to a fifth of a second at full aperture in lit corners.

There was no electronic flash as yet: it came later, around the time that Charles went into partnership with John of Clive Courtney's. I enjoyed the Sunday weddings, as groups were not set up traditionally outside the synagogue. It suited me to take the photographs by photoflood light at the reception. I would tootle around the churches on my bike, and on occasions I would leave a spare camera in my saddlebag outside the church. Again, pictures were taken at the reception by a single photoflood held by a guest.

I used a small rigid tripod, which was strapped to my crossbar. Two films of 16 on 120 film would cover the job. These would be developed and proofed and prints got back to the reception. On the Masonic functions Charles drove around in a little Austin 7 (he didn't need a driving test as he had driven a fire engine during the war).

Things really started to get busy, and business with the Masonics was booming. A steady tripod was used for guests arriving to ensure a perfect sharpness: I used photoflood as the main light source.

On dark nights all my travel had to be by bus or train. I would go back to the darkroom to print the proofs and take them to the salesgirls, and I would stay there and watch the cabaret. Many times I had to catch the last train home to Hammersmith (by the time I got home all my family had gone to bed), only to get up again at seven o'clock to cycle to work.

Charles opened a small studio in Gamages of Holborn: a small area for the studio was partitioned off in the toy department. I was the only operator and we became busy, mainly taking passport photos. Gamages was a lovely, cosy place to work, and Holborn seemed to be full of interesting people.

There were still food shortages, yet the Gamages staff canteen knocked up very tasty dinners.

I dealt with many of the artistes from the Sadler's Wells Ballet, as the theatre was just round the corner. All our photography was lit by two studio floods using a Rolleiflex with a 35 mm cine back. Lunchtime was our busiest time. An attraction for the studio was when Charles engaged one of his girl colourists to airgraph spray prints outside the studio entrance. One night many of the colour samples were stolen from the display.

When Charles moved to Soho Square a new director came into the company. The whole balance of working changed. Electronic flash had arrived and made photography a lot easier. It was time for me to go.

One of the first pictures to be taken of Charlie with the Woolworth camera - 1937.

Self-portrait taken using my mother's dusting cane to press the
shutter release on Ensign folding camera - 1941.

Me in A.T.C. uniform - 1940.

Phil Collins at home with his first drum kit.

Val Doonican – taken in studio at our home in Shepherds Bush.

Above: Pans People on *TOTP* with Clive Dunne.

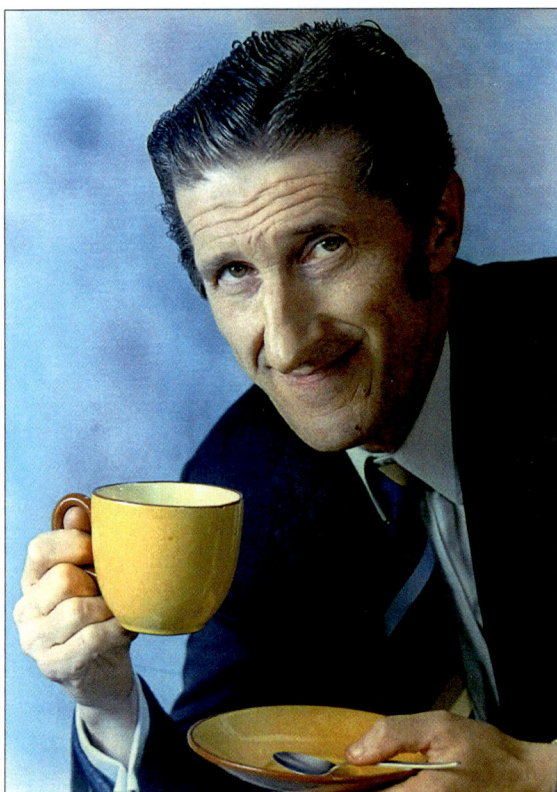

Left: Harry Goodwin with a cup of his favourite brew.

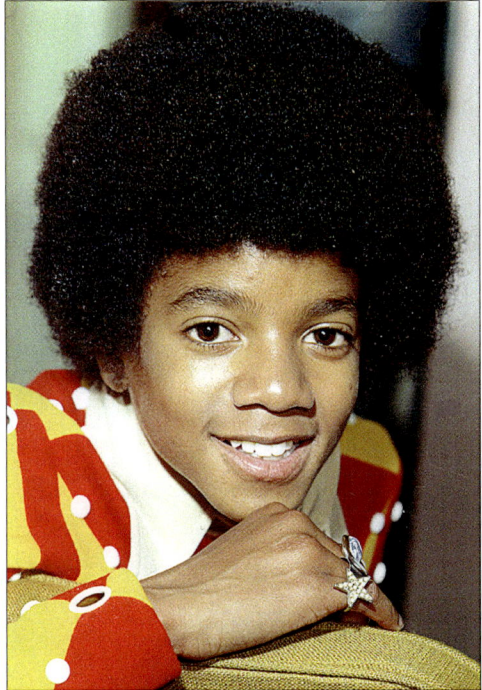

Michael Jackson on *TOTP*.

The Beatles on *TOTP* singing "Ticket to Ride".

George Mitchell (left) and George Inns (producer) -
The Black and White Minstrel Show.

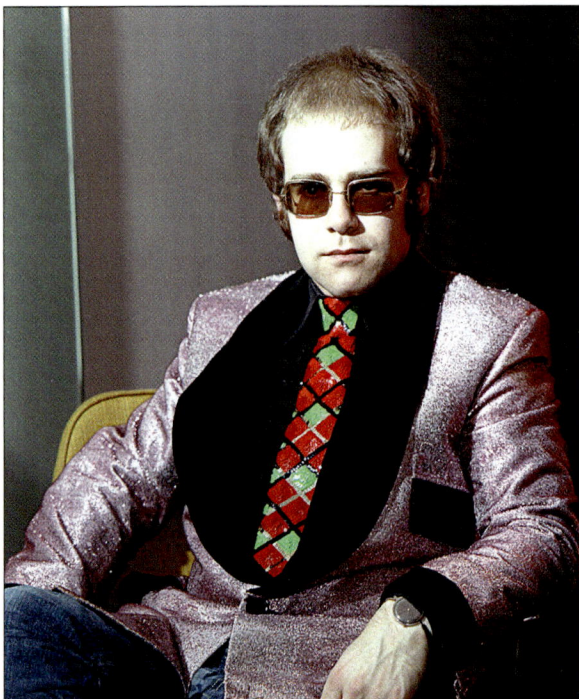

Elton John – before
going on *TOTP* to sing
"Crocodile Rock".

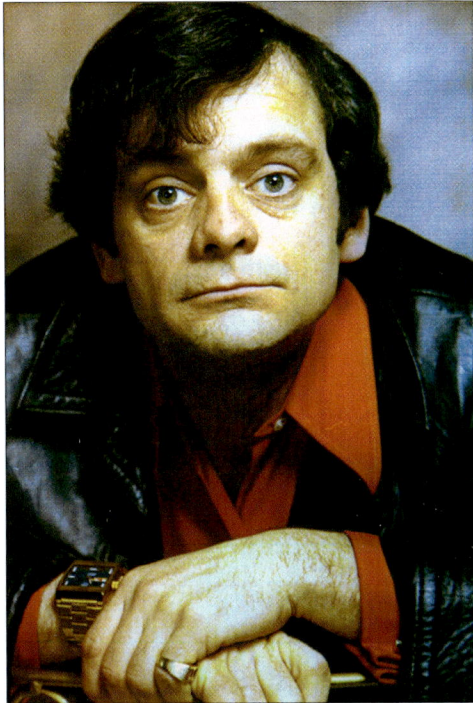

Sir David Jason as Del Boy.

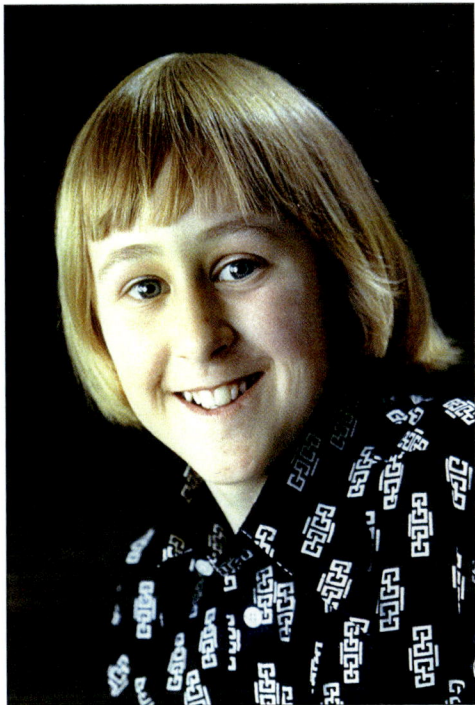

Nicholas Lyndhurst photographed whilst at Corona Stage School.

The Beatles – waiting on studio floor at *TOTP*.

Patrick Moore – "The Sky at Night" was broadcast one night from
our studio at home in Shepherds Bush.

CHAPTER SEVEN

I WAS OFFERED a partnership in a small company doing door-to-door photography, and it was a chance to work for myself at last: no more bosses. It was a challenge. There were two other partners who were always at loggerheads: this resulted in one dropping out, leaving me with one partner who wasn't a photographer but a very good salesman.

Alan was ten years older than me. Before the war he had been a salesman working for his brother, a stonemason in Wolverhampton. Alan had sold tombstones and his motto had been, 'Catch them with their insurance book in their hands and tears in their eyes.' He was very clever with words. We got on well together and he was a very good, honest friend.

The photography was very simple. Few people had cameras: the photographer would walk the streets with two canvassers, who would call when they had a take. I would then get the canvasser to hold up a photoflood while the photograph of the customer's child was taken. Sometimes – instead of using a photoflood – we used the light near the street door. I used the Leica 3A with an f2 Summar lens, and we would get fifteen to twenty customers a day. Postcard proofs would be printed and sold to the customer by a salesman a few days later. The main aim would be to sell the mother a large hand-coloured picture in a glass stand-up frame.

We managed to get hold of a super airgraph colourist named Freda. She came to work for us in our basement premises in Westbourne Park. This was also our darkroom. I was the printer. So it was three days on the road, then two days in the dark. It worked quite well for many months until a larger company asked us to process their rolls of film and we became darkroom slaves. This larger firm sold their photographic work to tallymen, who then introduced their own wares (like clothing and household sundries). We also took on processing prints from three local hospitals. This was well before hospitals had their own photographic departments.

We became very busy and moved to larger premises in Kentish Town, where we used more darkroom staff. We had the advantage of a showcase and a small studio, and as a result we attracted a few local portraits and weddings. The workplace was situated opposite Dunn & Co., the hat people. We became very friendly with this firm and began processing photographs of their shop window layout stills. Dunn & Co. had 200 shops.

Our landlord in Kentish Town was a perfumer, and he had his perfume factory on the ground floor and basement. We became fairly busy with passing trade and weddings, and I became very interested in pictorial photography at Hampshire House. It was one of the best London photography clubs, with a very well-known member – Mr Mark Oliver Dell, of Dell and Wainwright. There is nothing like having your pictures in a monthly competition and being judged.

The club moved from its original site in Hampshire Hog Lane to Westcott Lodge, a lovely old house standing right on the bank of the Thames. We did have the odd outing with Mr Dell around Strand-on-the-Green in Chiswick, but the most interesting classes were given by Geoffrey Phillips at his home in Chiswick. He would show us how to do bromoil transfer with our ready-bleached prints, and stipple away with brushes and oil paints. Mr Dell died of a stroke when holidaying in his beloved Pyrenees, and his cameras and pictures were auctioned at the Hammersmith Town Hall. I now regret not buying anything, especially his fine architectural 16 x 20 prints.

A very interesting speaker at the club was Tony Armstrong- Jones. He gave us a talk while his Chinese girlfriend sat cross-legged in yoga fashion at the back of the meeting. The club became so full that we moved to the small hall in Hammersmith Town Hall. All our work was black-and-white, and we had the very best speakers and judges around. What's more, because I was a member and had the advantage of an established darkroom I could buy all my paper and chemicals at trade prices.

There was much more critical judging when I first joined Hampshire House. Some prints were given as low a mark as two out of ten. There was much more anger and fire back then. I remember when a judge had to be rescued from the fireworks that followed his judgements. A speaker was asked once how he got this wonderful contrast in his prints, as there was always a mystery about development times. The question was asked, 'How long do you leave the film in the developer?' He replied, 'As long as it takes me to sit on the toilet.' These types of remarks were quite common. Nowadays no one seems to get less than seven out of ten.

Most photographers read the *Amateur Photographer*, as it was full of lively articles. They advertised a trip to Keukenhof bulb fields for ten pounds per person: the trip was arranged by Clarksons, a holiday company. My wife and I and our two young sons had to be at London airport early to get the full day in. Our money was changed at the Dutch airport into ten pound units, and away we went on a glorious coach trip. All our food was laid on in a hotel. We visited Rotterdam and The Hague and the bulb markets, and we arrived back home at 10 p.m. without a hitch. What a bargain at ten pounds!

Ernie Baker was our Kodak rep. He was also rep to the Armstrong-Jones studio on Shaftesbury Avenue. He once explained how he was bundled out of the Armstrong-Jones studio because Princess Margaret was on her way to see him. A few months later Ernie surprised us when he said that he had received an invitation to the wedding of Princess Margaret. Ernie and his wife had to be in their seat in Westminster Abbey at seven o'clock in the morning to fit in with the royal arrangements.

    Talking of the Thameside brings me to a very important time in my life.

CHAPTER EIGHT

IT WAS ON the Thameside that I met my wife to be, Joyce. She worked in the City for the Westminster Bank. I met her with a friend while she was supporting the Shell rowing eight. My eldest brother was a very keen oarsman: he was the one working in the Harrods furniture department, and he was the stroke of the Harrods boat for many years. I was rowing for the RAFA in the London Polytechnic boathouse and, being the lightest of the crew, I was always at bow. There is nothing as great as rowing on the Thames with eight other men on a Sunday morning in spring.

It was here at a regatta where I met my wife. She lived in the east end of London, in Plaistow. We met every other evening and travelled from each end of the District line to meet at Charing Cross. We wandered around the West End for an enjoyable four years, and we were married in 1952.

I booked seats at the London Palladium for every fortnightly change of programme. They were brilliant shows. We also took in all the American stage musicals: there was *South Pacific, Annie Get Your Gun, Carousel,* and *Oklahoma!.* We didn't miss any. What a great life. It was our engagement time.

We took out a mortgage on a house in Shepherd's Bush and moved in straight from our honeymoon in Cornwall. The house cost £1875. It eventually became our studio, and we lived there for forty-four years.

The popularity of television was creeping in and the camera club membership was falling off so we linked up with the Ealing camera club at Ealing Town Hall, renaming it the Ealing and Hampshire House Photographic Society (the EHHPS).

The darkroom side of our business in Kentish Town was also easing off – the staff were taking home better money than we were – so we had to lay off the printers and colourists. My colleague was offered a job managing a developing and printing factory in Putney. He took it, leaving me on my own. Kentish Town was quite a journey on my own, and as I was doing little work I decided to sell off most of the equipment to work in my own house in Shepherd's Bush. There were no overheads or rent to pay, but the processing side became very boring.

We were photographing the local stage school children, and decided that show business was to be our new line. We had a very large front room with high ceilings, and I fitted it out with lights and began studio photography. I had the back wall coved and the floor painted with hard-wearing floor paint, and the floor was covered with hardboard.

All I needed was customers. One can't put advertising showcases in the front garden – at least, not in a private house, especially when your neighbours are of good class and mainly business people. The idea was to contact people who had to come to you. I wrote to more stage schools and child model agencies. The stage school children had many interesting stories to tell, as many were working with the big stars of film and stage.

The model agency children were usually beautiful youngsters who were very easy to photograph because they had been trained on how to appear in front of a camera. One little five-year-old girl called Noriko Matsuoko was chosen to be the little princess who hid under Yul Brynner's robe in *The King and I*. While waiting in the wings for the entry of the other princesses Yul Brynner cleared his throat and spat on the floor. Noriko peered out from his skirt and watched all the other little girls walk through the spit and tread it all over the floor of the Palladium.

Noriko was with the Elisabeth Smith Child Model Agency, an agency that I had dealt with for over thirty years. One local stage school had many child stars, including Phil Collins and Jack Wild. Then came the Corona Academy, with Susan George, Dennis Waterman and Mark Lester, who played Oliver. Then came Aida Foster, Italia Conti and Sylvia Young.

The work was shared among many photographers. It kept me busy, and I was learning a great deal about portraiture. It is a pity that we had to have appointments: it meant that people had to come when maybe they didn't feel their best. I tried to fit these people in when they felt good. With children it is different. They are always ready: they don't have grown-up problems. Mind you, children coming straight from school can be full of excitement and can become difficult to work with.

They all thought they were going to be big stars, and many of them did become famous. I remember reading in the *British Journal of Photography* one week an article by the manager of an advertising firm which said that he would not employ a photographer over the age of thirty-five years. He stated that after that age they would have lost all their creativity ... quite a depressing thought.

I did fancy putting a small advert in *The Stage*. This did mean putting up with the usual prank calls from idiots. It did, however, also introduce me to pop groups. It was stated at the time that there were fifty thousand pop groups in the British Isles – five thousand in London alone. They were always messy: it meant bringing drum kits and setting up microphones.

When a group called the Five Dimensions came along Jimmy Powell said, 'Don't take many single shots of Rod Stewart. We are getting rid of him: we don't like the sound of his voice.' Phil Collins was a regular, because his mother was a partner in the Collins Speake stage school.

Jack Wild was in this school. One day Mrs Collins brought Jack along to be photographed in his Artful Dodger outfit. They had borrowed it from the studio wardrobe without permission. There was a great kerfuffle when they found out that it was missing, because the outfit was part of a museum collection. It was an antique and irreplaceable: filming could not continue without it.

Mitch Mitchell was another young drummer boy from the Corona school. When he came along with his drum kit we felt sure he would be famous. He joined Jimi Hendrix, so that came true.

Nicholas Lyndhurst was a friend of his at the school: he was famous in *Only Fools and Horses*. Anne Shelton (of wartime fame) was a lovely lady. So was Ruby Wax, who even now doesn't seem to look any older. Then there was Jeanette Charles, who was the Queen's lookalike. She was in many films. Bonnie Langford came along for pictures when she was going to sing and dance in the musical *Gypsy*. Her nieces Summer and Scarlett Strallen are now big stars in the world of dancing.

Many interesting artistes came along from the Paul Raymond Revuebar. There were striptease girls and many conjurors and illusionists, as well as dance groups. The *QE2* dancers came to see us in between their trips on the liner. They were lovely tall girls. They would fill our hallway with boas, garlands and dresses. When the ship was in dock I went on board to photograph them. However, we then made a decision to reduce some of our workload as the travelling and setting up of some of the acts could be very time-consuming, so we focused on the children and the stage schools.

We had a lovely changing room, and the children could be booked for every hour – and no make-up needed. I had my little pink pencil to blot out any spots on their face. The appointments were more positive, and they meant that my wife and I could have good shopping days in the West End. The shops were easily reachable by car along the new Western Avenue motorway. Oxford Street could take fifteen minutes: parking then was fairly easy.

Many actors came for *Spotlight* sessions (*Spotlight* was a photographic directory of stage school students, and was used by agencies who were seeking to fill vacancies for TV, theatre and film roles). It was a fairly quick and easy task: one roll of film. The idea with actors was to make a good portrait that represented the actor realistically – not too glamorous, because they had to be assessed again in their natural face for an audition. They had to look like their face in *Spotlight*.

I had to give up my precious Hasselblad: the clop of the mirror rising before the shutter was causing too many blinks. Also the flash socket was indecisive: it gave bad connections through the flash link. So I changed to twin-lens Mamiyaflex: the image of the sitter could be viewed continuously, and there were no flash delays with the between-lens shutter. That meant no delays in exposure.

My good friend Harold Fountain of St Albans adapted my camera to take a 16-exposure back, and with a little juggling and filing of the back I was able to get seventeen lovely fat frames from a roll of film. This was a colossal saving, because the use of the image was equivalent to the square format.

Harold designed and made (with the help of David White Engineering) a complete camera body with a revolving back. We called it the Albanflex. This became my main camera.

The 120 films were never cut to put them in packets: this meant that numbering them was easier. I managed to contact-print them in three bites. As there were no negative bags the films were stored and filed naked in long boxes. The enlarging and counting of frame numbers was also made easier.

My advert in *The Stage* was due to run out when I had a phone call that was about to change my life.

CHAPTER NINE

THE TOP OF the Pops photographer Harry Goodwin had noticed my tiny advert. Because the phone number was prefixed with SHE this told him that I was situated in Shepherd's Bush. He phoned me to ask if he could borrow my darkroom to process his two and a quarter inch square lantern slides that he used for back projection on *TOTP*. We dismissed the call as a possible prankster on the telephone, but when Harry turned up the next day in the pouring rain and soaked through we could never have realised how our life was going to change to the exciting life that was as yet to come.

Harry had just photographed Sonny and Cher, and needed to develop his films as soon as possible to make his lantern slides. He had brought along his own MQ developer and a box of slides. He had used his Yashica Mat twin lens reflex camera with a Yashinon 80 mm lens. His method of developing was very unorthodox – at least, it was a new one to me.

His film was Ilford FP3, and the developer was warmed up to sixty-eight degrees. Harry would then light up a cigarette, close the darkroom door and run the film see-saw fashion through the developer. After a few minutes in the dark he would draw on the cigarette to make it glow and gauge the image density coming through the back of the film. When visually correct – by the light of the cigarette – the film would be rinsed and fixed. We may smile at this method, but Harry was a perfectionist. He got it just right every time.

Harry aimed at a fairly dense contrasty negative that needed a soft paper. This gave him glamorous-looking prints that didn't need retouching or spotting. This method was taking far too long, especially when a number of films were involved. The time-and-temperature developing tank had to be the alternative. Harry soon changed over to it.

Most of Harry's pictures were taken by a Mecablitz electronic flash. He changed to a Braun flash so that he could use an extension flash like mine. The extension flash – when held behind the sitter on the wall – would knock out the shadow caused by the frontal light. He was never short of assistance.

Harry's camera needed to be changed. It would only focus down to three feet. The 80 mm lens gave very small heads, which meant that the enlarger lamp house was on the top of its column, and shaking. I myself would take a roll of colour film the same time as Harry, using a split lead when using our umbrella flash. These colour films would be sent to odd magazines and processed by them. They were useful for advertising the show.

When he saw the lovely large heads on the Mamiyaflex he soon changed his camera. The parallax took some getting used to, and the 13.5 lens proved to be our best focal length. Harry had been the show's photographer for eighteen months already: they had been using a church hall in Manchester before coming to London.

Johnnie Stewart (the *TOTP* producer) asked around if anyone up there could recommend a stills photographer who didn't watch the clock and who could work on the show. Harry was the ideal: he was already covering the Harry Worth shows and *The Good Old Days* with Barney Colehan, who had recommended him. Johnnie needed someone available at all times.

Johnnie Stewart was a pre-war sound producer. He was producing a TV programme called *The Trad Fad ... and All That Jazz* when he said to the BBC planners, 'Why not do a programme featuring the top twenty record hits?' He was told to get it together and the programme would be his.

Johnnie himself was a master piano player.

My photographic task was to produce the lantern slide featuring a picture of the artiste or pop group in the charts. I would also mount up Harry's print of the singer on a 12 x 10 card. The caption would have a large Letraset number denoting its position in the charts.

The back projection unit was run by a private company. The projector was a massive, long machine. The extra-brilliant light bulbs cost thirty-six pounds each – a lot of money in the 1960s. These three and a quarter inch square slides were very easy for me to make – they were the standard size used for all camera club competitions. At the Regent Street Polytechnic I also learned how to finish every slide with a quick bath in caustic soda after developing. This gave a nice contrasty edge to the image, which made the whole picture stand out.

Everything was black-and-white: no colour yet. So here I was (with my own camera) meeting the really big stars by Harry's side. The first lady that I had to record was Petula Clark. Harry wasn't keen on confronting her. She had been disappointed in the last picture used and, being another perfectionist, wanted to edit every shot taken. I had to shoot the pictures over the backs of a group of Japanese journalists interviewing her on tape for one of their pop magazines. It was slightly unnerving at the beginning, because you were confronting famous people. Harry would say, 'Once you shut that dressing room door they are just the same people as we are.'

The show had moved from Manchester into the Lime Grove Studios in Shepherd's Bush. One of the first artistes to perform at Lime Grove was Arthur Brown, who tried to set the studios alight with his version of 'Fire'. The studios had large sound stages (I am told) for the shooting of such famous films as *The Lady Vanishes*, with Alfred Hitchcock directing. *TOTP* was still in black-and-white while we were waiting for the change to colour in the new studios in Wood Lane.

When we were schoolboys we would wait for hours for celebrities to come out of Lime Grove Studios so that we could grab their autographs. All the dressing rooms were quite old and very large, with fanlights.

So far *TOTP* only occupied two evenings of my time. I had my own little studio at home to look after, and a continuous run of children booked. My wife would always be on the phone to remind me of the appointments booked and the children waiting. It was a good job that I lived less than a mile away.

Harry was furious one evening when Gary Brooker of Procol Harum blocked him from taking photographs of their band. They had their own photographer, and Harry sat on the chair outside their dressing room waiting for the session to finish. We could see the flashes through the fanlight. Boy, what a night that was.

All the Americans were superb. They were well aware that they were ambassadors of their great country. Stevie Wonder would say, after you had finished taking his picture, 'Hey, hand me that camera and let me take a picture of you.' When he had got the camera he would then say, 'Which lens do I look through?'

When I talk to people now about the show I am asked, 'Who was your favourite?' I would say, 'Karen Carpenter.' She had a grand aura of loveliness; she had great respect for the people around her who were responsible for her fame. She would even thank you for taking her photograph.

Harry without a doubt would say, 'Muhammad Ali.' There could never be anyone like him. He lit the place up with his personality and presence. He enjoyed meeting all the canteen staff and commissionaires. Harry had him punching chins and posing with the ladies. In fact Harry rang John Conteh – our own boxing champion – to see if he was interested in meeting Ali. John lived in Liverpool. He jumped in his Jag and was on his way. He said he averaged ninety miles an hour along the motorway to get to the BBC on time.

Richard Drewett (the producer of *Parkinson*) knew Harry was mad keen on boxing, so Harry stayed over for an extra day. There was a great swell of photographers and photography in general about this time. Almost every other large firm had its own photographic unit. I found this out when I attended night school to improve my knowledge on the medical side and on portraiture in general. Walter Marynowicz ran a good portrait class at the Ealing School of Art. He was a master at lighting faces. He would set up the lights and leave us for a couple of hours to photograph ourselves. The main focus of learning was the Regent Street Polytechnic when Margaret Harker was in charge.

One unforgettable character was Malcolm Hoare, of banking fame. He was in charge of silver recovery in the Rank film laboratories. Then there was Richard Farrand of ICI who taught at the polytechnic and who was renowned as a classic arranger of objects. He also had a brilliant lad as an assistant. Then of course there were the Americans, who came over to show us how it should be done. They always seemed to be one jump ahead of us, with their super colour prints and creative ideas.

Rocky Gunn and Monty Zucker showed us how to photograph a wedding. They could spread wedding photography over a week. They worked with four or five assistants, and would arrange much of the photography before the wedding at a special day in a colourful area or seascape. Over here we are inclined to cram everything into one day because of our unreliable weather. There was Bill Stockwell with his 'misty' photographs and superimposed wedding shots. Rocky Gunn lived on hamburgers and Coca-Cola. They were obviously responsible for his heart attack. If I had to pick out one of our best portrait men I would say Eric Lawe of Northampton. Eric was the only man I knew who could arrange hands so that they looked natural.

CHAPTER TEN

MEANWHILE THE SHOW at home had to go on. My main photography now was the model agency children and stage school pupils. My trusty Albion flex was working overtime. Children were booked for hourly sessions. Usually I exposed two rolls of Tri-X film – that is, thirty-four exposures. All the work was black-and-white, though at the end of a session I would grab a few shots on colour film.

I was a member of the BIPP (the British Institute of Professional Photography) and needed colour prints to enter for associateship and fellowship qualifications. This was essential to make you improve your work.

Colour printing was just becoming available to the home user. I made my prints on Kodak colour paper on a Durst enlarger and developed them using a 16 x 20 drum processor. The print was held on a blanket to the heated drum that passed through a shallow tray of developer. It was long-winded, but ideal at the time.

To give you an idea of how awkward and costly it was to make prints ... Kodak sold Flexichrome dyes to smear over your dry prints, which would bring any unwanted hues back to normal. It was tricky, and I am indebted to the Agfa-Gevaert classes in Regent Street for my first tuition. We were told that jumping from black-and-white to colour was like driving a car on flat roads, then piloting a plane when you had to account for up and down movements.

I can remember (as well) going to an advanced colour class at Johnson's of Hendon, when we had to unscrew our Durst enlarger baseboard to assemble it again for a day-long lesson. When I came to process my 16 x 12 colour prints for fellowship entry I folded the paper over gently so that I could immerse it crossways in deep developer in a three-gallon tank. This was heated by a glass fish tank heater. I jiggled the print around with rubber gloves on.

I cannot praise the Kodak paper enough – indeed, all their material was superior. These prints have been framed, and adorn the walls of my house even now. The colour is as good as the day I made them nearly fifty years ago. There is no sign of fading. That is more than I can say about present computer inks: they don't last six months on a wall that receives bright light.

We had marvellous print criticism meetings at Paul Kaye's studio in Baker Street. Paul Kaye himself got this meeting together to try and catch up with the Americans. It was the best thing for us all. The critics were very severe – after all, we were charging for the photographs.

One of the main advantages was to see the work of other photographers. They came from all over London. Paul Kaye himself was a master at planning groups. He started by standing outside baby clinics and catching the mothers when they came with the children. In the next road, Lisson Grove, was the Sea Shell – the greatest fish and chip shop in the whole world. It was worth queuing up for an hour with all the celebrities for skate and chips.

Meanwhile, the BBC was moving *TOTP* from Lime Grove to the Wood Lane Studios. The change was from black-and-white to colour. The studio lighting was not all that bright, it seemed. I needed a thirtieth of a second at f2 on my Nikkormat 35 mm camera to record the pop groups. I would be using Kodak 35 mm cine colour negative stock. This film at 100 ASA was plentiful because the BBC outside broadcast cameramen had odd ends in their cases. It processed easily in a normal colour film developer. Its sooty anti-halation backing was easily removed with cotton wool.

In Lime Grove we had the dressing room next to David Coleman, the sports presenter. This time he also moved over next to us and demanded Harry's dressing room, which was a lot bigger. Jimmy Savile was on the other side. His dressing room door was always open, and the loud noise of laughter and chatting could be heard all over. We were never aware of any problems. The commissionaires were very strict at letting the youngsters in the studio door. A nurse was always on hand.

In fact a whole team of Americans came over to produce the Carol Burnett shows. They were full of appreciation of the good things they learned at the BBC. The sheer quality of the place and their comfort in working there was good to hear about.

Many of the popular people on television had a chance to sing on *TOTP*. There was Frankie Howerd, Ken Dodd, Dick Emery, Spike Milligan, and even our little Jack Wild. They all had their own singing number to put over.

Ken Dodd had been in the charts for six weeks on *TOTP* with 'Tears'. His next number to follow was 'The River'. Out of all the sketches that Ken Dodd made for TV little would he know that he would be creating his most laughable situation when he was asked to record his song on the River Thames.

Cecil Korer got the job. A pleasure steamer was hired by the BBC. The thing was to get Ken to mime the song while the boat was passing the Houses of Parliament. On the first run they lost lip sync, so the boat had to turn round on full tide to do another run. The next time Ken's hair blew up all over his face, so ... another run. The next time the crew of a passing tug hooted when they saw what was going on... Six times the steamer had to make the run. Meanwhile, every time it turned it sent up waves to rock and disturb the boats moored on the Thameside. The phone to the captain rang continuously to report damage to private craft. There was panic and pandemonium. Eventually we managed to get it right.

I photographed Jack's wedding when he married Gaynor Jones, who was a pupil at his stage school. Gaynor was one of the prettiest brides I have ever photographed. She sang in a trio with Lulu's sister. They both lived happily nearby in Chiswick.

Jack had two monkeys. One would jump on your shoulder when you entered his house and would preen your hair strand by strand until Jack brushed him off. They were real devils. Bit by bit they had stripped their large playroom of all its wallpaper.

The move to the television centre meant other changes – for instance, the musicians' union was insisting that there could be no more miming to backing tracks. This meant that the orchestra had to be brought in to cover the chart records and that changes had to be made because the stars would be singing on a live programme. All these adjustments were taken care of by Dickie Chamberlain, the BBC sound specialist, who had to reorganise the whole sound system.

Johnny Pearson was to be the orchestra arranger and conductor. Johnny had to listen to the pop artistes' records to assess how many violins, trumpets, pianos and guitars would be needed for that week's programme. The group Blue Mink was formed from his orchestra. Johnny spent all night working out the orchestration and arrangement. The band was full of great lads. I recommended our local fish and chip shop in Chiswick, and after the show they filled it to the brim every week.

The Rolling Stones were easy to get pictures of. Mick Jagger was always the perfect gentleman: this is how Harry assessed groups. There were our favourite groups, like the Hollies, the Tremeloes and T.Rex with Marc Bolan. When they came in the Beatles had their own special guards and were able to bounce into the studio to sing 'Ticket to Ride'. We had a good session in their dressing room afterwards – not bad, considering that they must have had many other photocalls that day.

Linda Eastman was a freelance photographer. She was one of the many press people allowed into *TOTP* for the run-through rehearsal. Harry allowed Linda to leave her Hasselblad cameras in his dressing room while she danced on the show. One day she said, 'I am going to a dinner party tonight, and I shall be sitting next to Paul McCartney.' That was the beginning of a fine romance.

Harry's pictures of the Beatles have become famous: I am glad that he signed my copies. My sons always say that you can tell a Harry Goodwin picture a mile off. It is true: you can. Of course the secret was to press the button at the right moment.

There were times when we would take the same person. We would use our split lead coupled to a flash umbrella – and although our contact sheets looked pretty much the same for both of us, I noticed that Harry had many more shots ticked off than mine.

One thing unshakeably sound about Harry was that he didn't touch alcohol. Nor did he pester or even touch his glamorous models, yet he still got the poses right. We had both our addresses on notepaper and cards. Therefore if a beauty queen knocked on the door asking for Harry, my wife would say, 'Harry is not here. Would Ron be okay to take your pictures?' 'No,' they would say. 'We want Harry.'

In the BBC canteen one evening I heard a cashier call across to another cashier, 'There are some beautiful girls in here tonight. What show are they on?' Of course they would be Harry's girls. They would come down from up north to see Harry and dance on *TOTP*. There was something about his tenacity and concentration which made me realise that he was aiming at something special. Harry always announced that he had a winner or a Rembrandt, whoever he had before the camera.

Many inserts were made for *TOTP* midweek, to take in artistes who could not make the show's scheduled time. One of these was James Brown. He was a very nice man. He carried a pocketful of gold rings that he would place on the fingers of his young girl fans in the audience.

James started his recording, and halfway through his singing he was halted by the producer because a camera was out of position. James didn't take kindly to the interruption: his dignity had been damaged. He walked off the set and out of the studio door, jumped into his chauffeured car and sped off. The poor producer stepped down from his box, bewildered. He could not understand what had happened.

Dusty Springfield will never be forgotten. She was always difficult to get pictures of, but could easily be forgiven when she sang with that beautiful voice. She put everything she had into her songs. Another fine singer was Shirley Bassey. She would wind up her breathing in the wings and give out her version of 'Fool on the Hill' on stage.

Don Maclean sang 'Vincent' with a group of young fans placed around him. There was no orchestra – just Don and his guitar. It was a quiet number. After he had finished the recording a sound man came round to me and said, 'Ron, the clonk of your camera shutter came right on a low note in the song. If I can't block it out Johnnie Stewart will go mad.' Fortunately nothing more was said. It made me change to my dear old Leica with its silent shutter, but only for that day.

Cecil Korer was an assistant producer on *TOTP* with Johnnie Stewart. He scanned the BBC workboards one day and saw that they wanted a programme producer for a quiz show called *Ask the Family*, with Robert Robinson in the chair. Cecil applied and got the job as the producer. He then asked me to become the resident photographer.

My job there was to photograph everyday objects in close-up. They had to be cunningly arranged and not easily recognised, even when the studio camera zoomed out. I worked closely with Eric Illett, who did the animation and cartoons. We had a wonderful time thinking up ideas. Eric took over from the old animator, Alfred Wurmser. His hobby was cutting out mouldings for Airfix plastic toys.

The best part of the day was in the hospitality room, when Robert would chat about his tangles with Denis Norden and Frank Muir on *Call My Bluff*. Two of the quiz programmes would be recorded on one Sunday afternoon. I continued with the programme for fifteen years: I was happy to see my name mentioned on the roller caption.

Ask the Family had a spot on the programme whereby the camera opened up on a section of a celebrity's face. As the camera zoomed out the person became more recognisable: it was up to the families on the show to guess who it was first.

I had by now got to know many of the producers in light entertainment at the BBC. *Parkinson* was a programme with many celebrities. I had already got to know Michael Parkinson when I visited his house on the Thames at Bray. They were doing his life story even then.

The producer Richard Drewett gave me the all-clear to photograph anybody on the show. When Bing Crosby was on the show the floor manager said, 'He is on his own. Knock on the door and ask if you can take a few shots of him on *Parkinson*.' I was feeling quite sensitive and felt myself vibrating like a pneumatic drill – for here I was, speaking to an icon of my schooldays. He was very sensitive to the camera catching him without his hat on, so I put the camera away. It was one of my greatest days. I spoke to him for a good twenty minutes.

Orson Welles was an all-time great. The word was that he was a bit fiery and maybe difficult, but when he came in everything was okay. I also got to know Val Doonican pretty well. I went to his house in Rickmansworth many times. I would pop along to the Shepherd's Bush Empire during the rehearsals of Val's famous guests. The Empire was just down the road, and parking was always easy. I would rush home to get a few small prints ready for Val, which he would collect on the same night after the show. The neighbours would be watching.

Terry Hughes began the first Val Doonican shows. Terry turned out to be brilliant. He then started to produce *The Two Ronnies*. He was so good on these shows that the Americans grabbed him. Stan Dorfman was an ex-designer at the BBC. He was an assistant producer of *TOTP*, along with Johnnie Stewart. Stan then had his own programmes producing the Bobby Gentry shows. His designer talent was released in his work. He aimed at making his shows have great visual acuity, and kept the audience's eye entertained with magnetic visuals. Stan said, 'Even when switching channels the viewer may be attracted to a compelling eye-catching picture.'

Johnnie Stewart once said, 'Next week we have got the Bee Gees. They will be bigger than the Beatles.' He could be right, for when they went to America it was reckoned that they were earning a million pounds a day.

When the Osmonds came over from America they were asked first to make a recording in a small BBC cinema theatre in Regent Street. The boys had not slept for three days, and went to sleep in the front rows with their full make-up on. They were true professionals, for when woken they jumped up straight on to the stage to mime to 'Crazy Horses'.

Another programme I did the captions for was *Dee Time*. Simon Dee had his own photographer (Dezo Hoffman). There was one time when Gypsy Rose Lee was a guest. The producer asked me to keep her talking in the dressing room while Jerry Lewis and Vincent Price imitated her dance routine by performing a mock striptease to her famous music. She was furious when the sound reached her. She rushed upstairs to the studio but, fortunately, ended up quite amused. Some of the greats on *Dee Time* were Stéphane Grapelli, Yehudi Menuhin and Candice Bergen.

Diana Dors married Alan Lake at Caxton Hall. I photographed the wedding. Dee Time paid for the reception, provided that Diana and Alan came to be interviewed by Simon Dee on the programme.

On *Dee Time* I was introduced to Captain Richard Clayton. He was talking to Simon about the Royal Navy Presentation tour of our diminishing navy. The captain invited me to take a few shots on board his own battleship.

Ladies were not allowed on board. While waiting for me my wife was shown over *HMS Victory* by a young sailor.

A nice little job I had was when a good journalist friend had to prepare a booklet featuring Ladbrokes Hotels in Malta. My wife and I had the very pleasant task of providing photographs of the hotel's activities. We had to make sure that we did not include couples who might not want to be seen together, especially in the gaming saloon. We were treated like royalty by the hotel staff. We had a hearty breakfast one day and soon after it we were invited round to our wine waiter's house for a further meal of lampuki pie, including a large glass of strong beer. We were already full up and the weather was so hot but we could not offend Joe's wife, who had spent hours preparing this spread. We were in agony afterwards, and could hardly get back to our hired car. They were such a kind-hearted couple.

I must butt in with a bit of fanciful writing about holidays abroad, when I can mention New York. It should be part of everybody's education to afford themselves a few days in the most vibrant city in the world. We have made a few visits. The last was when Hurricane Floyd hit New York, and the next day left the pavements strewn with blown-out umbrellas. A visit to the Bowery filled in the gaps in all my boyhood memories of the Dead End Kids and Humphrey Bogart.

A good programme was assembled quickly when Ray Charles's management rang the BBC to say that they were in Britain, and, 'Are you interested in recording a show?' When the BBC said there would be no time for rehearsals, Ray Charles said, 'Who needs rehearsals?' So a one and a half hour show was recorded off the cuff and split into two marvellous programmes.

Harry and I were invited to take pictures of the Black and White Minstrels. This show was the baby of George Inns, who was a sound producer with Johnnie Stewart before the war. The singing and music was pre-recorded in the sound studios at Marble Arch and acted out in number 8 studios in

Wood Lane. We all know what a beautiful show that was.

Alan Bell took over producing the show when George Inns died. He was so good that he was offered *Last of the Summer Wine* and stayed on that until its end. Georgie Fame did get fame when he sang with the Count Basie orchestra. The Count reckoned that he was as good as any of the famous singers that had fronted the band. Georgie, I know, was in his element – for here he had the lovely tight sound of the Basie orchestra backing him. The mikes had to be tuned in to every single instrument. The *In Concert* shows were recorded at the London Hippodrome. Vic Damone was asked in rehearsals to sing some of his numbers (so as to time the show). Come the evening he had no voice left. The audience had to come back three days later.

It was on this show that I got to speak to George Harrison. He had brought Billy Preston, the organist, over from America. George felt that he could become a big name. George was a man of few words. When I told him that I had become interested in yoga and had been to the ashram in North London that he had funded his curt reply was, 'I have nothing to do with them any more.'

At the BBC *Dad's Army* was a very popular show. One episode called for the use of a Smith Gun. It was just a long tube that would even fire a bottle of Guinness. A copy had to be made for the programme. I went with a production assistant to the Imperial War Museum store in Kent to photograph one. This was an old aircraft hangar that had thousands of relics of World War Two. I got very interested in reading some of the Japanese and American leaflets dropped by their aircraft. They were very rude and very comical.

Charlie, my old schoolmate, was still appearing on my pictures. He was a scenery foreman at the BBC. He would look in our dressing room door and ask if there were any bits of background that might be useful, as all scenery was fireproof and smelt of cats. My house already ponged from the smell of chemicals.

There were many interesting shows at the BBC. One was the Tutankhamen exhibition at the British Museum. I was told to arrive at 8 a.m.. Even then all the car parking spaces were full. One of the attendants found me a spot at the back of the museum. I was not allowed to touch any of the artefacts to be photographed. Young Egyptian girls with gloved hands would move the pieces under the camera, and all this was going with the eyes of the famous golden mask peering down on you. There was a voodoo effect. I hardly remember driving home.

Then there was the *So You Think...?* series produced by Cecil Korer. One called for some Cliff Michelmore doubles to turn up. Twenty-two arrived. Shakira Baksh was on the *Where in the World?* show before she married Michael Caine. Then there was a series of charity shows, which included the marvellous Malcolm Muggeridge. Every word that Malcolm uttered was magical. So too was the voice of Joan Bakewell.

One week a studio could not be found to record The Sky at Night. Even the weather forecast studios were booked up, so I was asked if they could borrow my studio. The neighbours were surprised when two large outside broadcast vans turned up in front of our house and ran heavy cables through the front door. I will always remember Patrick Moore for his brilliant memory. He never forgot a face.

CHAPTER ELEVEN

It was time to move from our lovely old house in Shepherd's Bush. The whole area was changing. We didn't have a garage, and when QPR were playing we had to leave our car a good half mile away. The vicarage was opposite our house. For a long time the vicar thought that the odd flashes of light that crept over his curtains were from the trains on the nearby Central line.

A hairdresser who lived next door said one day, 'I've seen some rare old fruit go into your place.' No doubt he was referring to the *QE2* dancers. They were all beautiful six-footers.

We live in Bournemouth now. Our house was newly built. I had a darkroom and one large room with extra light sockets for a studio. We only had one customer make the hundred-mile journey.

I am still asked to photograph the odd musical for a local opera society. Everything is digital now: no more smelly chemicals. I use a Panasonic f150 with the trusty Leica lens. It is hopeless for photographing children due to shutter delay, and that seems to be the bogey of all digital cameras.

Since we moved I have been a member of the Ferndown Camera Club (a very friendly club). Harry Goodwin has become a legendary figure in the world of pop photography, and has had many fine exhibitions.

At the Victoria & Albert museum his photographs were a great success. We met Pan's People, with Dee Dee, Ruth and Babs. Even Gary Leeds, drummer of the Walker Brothers, turned up. It is true what Harold

Young at Harrods said: 'There is not a great deal of money to be made in photography, unless you are at the top.'

Our wealth has been our lovely family. What a great life it has been!